How to use this book 

Follow the advice, in italics, where given.
Support the children as they read the text that is shaded in cream.
***Praise** the children at every step!*
Detailed guidance is provided in the Read Write Inc. Phonics Handbook.
Activity 8 (Answer the 'questions to read and answer') only appears in Sets 4–7.

8 reading activities

Children:

1 Practise reading the speed sounds.
2 Read the green and red words for the non-fiction text.
3 Listen as you read the introduction.
4 Discuss the vocabulary check with you.
5 Read the non-fiction text.
6 Re-read the non-fiction text and discuss the 'questions to talk about'.
7 Re-read the non-fiction text with fluency and expression.
9 Practise reading the speed words.

Speed sounds

Consonants *Say the pure sounds (do not add 'uh').*

f	l ll	m	n	r	s ss	v	z s	sh	**(th)**	ng nk

b	c k **(ck)**	d	g **(gg)**	h	j	p	qu	t	w **(wh)**	x	y	ch **(tch)**

Vowels *Say the vowel sound and then the word, e.g. 'a', 'at'.*

at	hen	in	on	up	day	see	high	blow	zoo

Each box contains one sound but sometimes more than one grapheme. Focus graphemes are ***circled****.*

Green words

Read in Fred Talk (pure sounds).

crack	stuck	catch	hatch	chest	silk
plant	kept	trap	them	egg	when

Read in syllables.

ab` do` men → abdomen

Read the root word first and then with the ending.

leg → legs   spin → spins   insect → insects   egg → eggs

Red words

the be are to or* look*

out* spider* spiderlings*

*red for this book only

Spiders

Introduction

Have you ever seen a spider up close? Do you know how many legs they have? What do you think about spiders? In this book you will learn about how they are born and how they find their food.

Written by Gill Munton

Vocabulary check

Discuss the meaning (as used in the non-fiction text) after the children have read the word.

	definition
abdomen	*the part of the body where the stomach is*
silk	*a very fine, strong thread*
sac	*a thin pouch for holding eggs*
hatch	*when a baby creature comes out of its egg*

Punctuation to note:

Let's The	*Capital letters that start sentences*
.	*Full stop at the end of each sentence*
!	*Exclamation mark*
,	*Comma to show a pause*
:	*Colon to show that a list is next*

Let's look at spiders!

A spider has:

- 8 legs
- a chest
- an abdomen.

leg

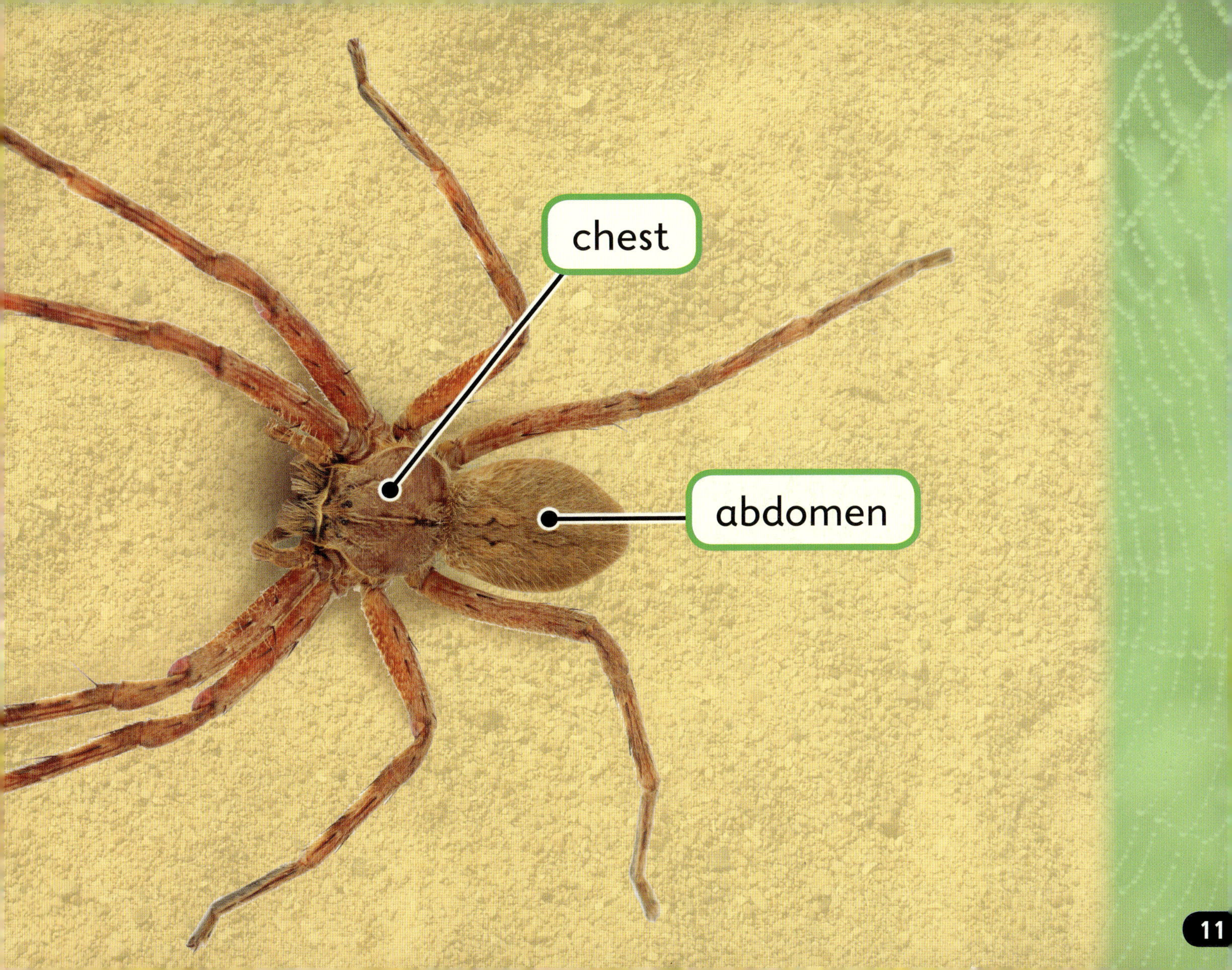
chest
abdomen

A spider spins a silk web.

It can be on a plant
or in a crack.

The web is an insect trap.

Insects get stuck in it and then the spider can catch them.

Up to 250 spider eggs are kept in an egg sac.

When the eggs hatch, spiderlings run out.

Questions to talk about 

Re-read the page. Read the question to the children. Tell them whether it is a FIND IT *question or* PROVE IT *question.*

FIND IT	**PROVE IT**
✓ *Turn to the page*	✓ *Turn to the page*
✓ *Read the question*	✓ *Read the question*
✓ *Find the answer*	✓ *Find your evidence*
	✓ *Explain why*

Page 10:	FIND IT	*How many legs does a spider have?*
Page 12:	FIND IT	*What does a spider spin?*
Page 13:	FIND IT	*Where can you find a spider web?*
Pages 14–15:	PROVE IT	*Why is a spider web useful?*
Page 16:	FIND IT	*Where are spider eggs kept?*

Speed words

Children practise reading the words across the rows, down the columns and in and out of order clearly and quickly.

leg	crack	run	chest	silk
kept	get	spin	catch	them
egg	stuck	trap	plant	has
when	can	hatch	then	web